To

_____

_____

From

_____

_____

To my little ones,

for every time I kissed them goodnight… B.V.

Written and compiled by Sophie Piper
Illustrations copyright
© 2011 Barbara Vagnozzi
This edition copyright
© 2011 Lion Hudson

The moral rights of the author
and illustrator have been asserted

A Lion Children's Book
an imprint of
Lion Hudson plc
Wilkinson House, Jordan Hill Road,
Oxford OX2 8DR, England
www.lionhudson.com
ISBN 978 0 7459 6151 4

First edition 2011
10 9 8 7 6 5 4 3 2 1 0

Acknowledgments
Every effort has been made to trace
and contact copyright owners for
material used in this book. We apologize
for any inadvertent omissions or errors.

All unattributed prayers are by Sophie
Piper and Lois Rock, copyright
© Lion Hudson.
Prayers by Mark Robinson and Victoria
Tebbs are copyright © Lion Hudson.
Prayer by Mother Teresa (p.23) used by
permission.
Carmina Gadelica collected by Alexander
Carmichael is published by
Floris Books, Edinburgh.

Bible extracts are taken or adapted
from the Good News Bible, published
by The Bible Societies/HarperCollins
Publishers Ltd, copyright © American
Bible Society 1966, 1971, 1976, 1992,
used by permission.
The Lord's Prayer (p.92) from *Common
Worship: Services and Prayers for the Church
of England* (Church House Publishing,
2000) is copyright © The English
Language Liturgical Consultation, 1988
and is reproduced by permission of the
publishers.

A catalogue record for this book is
available from the British Library

Typeset in 13/16 Old Claude
Printed in China November 2010
(manufacturer LH06)

Distributed by:
UK: Marston Book Services Ltd, PO
Box 269, Abingdon, Oxon OX14 4YN
USA: Trafalgar Square Publishing, 814
N Franklin Street, Chicago, IL 60610
USA Christian Market: Kregel
Publications, PO Box 2607, Grand
Rapids, MI 49501

God Bless Me

Sophie Piper

Illustrated by
Barbara Vagnozzi

LION
CHILDREN'S

CONTENTS

SAYING PRAYERS

I

Here I am beneath the sky
and all alone in prayer;
but I know God is listening,
for God is everywhere.

Lord, teach a little child to pray,
And then accept my prayer,
Thou hearest all the words I say
For thou art everywhere.

A little sparrow cannot fall
Unnoticed, Lord, by thee,
And though I am so young and small
Thou dost take care of me.

Teach me to do the thing that's right,
And when I sin, forgive,
And make it still my chief delight
To serve thee while I live.

JANE TAYLOR (1783–1824)

3

I close my eyes
and try to pray
but daydreams steal
my prayers away.
May some good angel
come close by
and take my prayers
to God on high.

4

O let us feel you very near
When we kneel down to pray.
Let us be still that you may send
A message for today.

ANONYMOUS

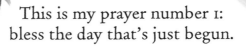

5

This is my prayer number 1:
bless the day that's just begun.

This is my prayer number 2:
may the sky be clear and blue.

This is my prayer number 3:
God, please take good care of me.

This is my prayer number 4:
help me love you more and more.

This is my prayer number 5:
make me glad to be alive.

This is my prayer number 6:
help me when I'm in a fix.

This is my prayer number 7:
make this world a bit like heaven.

This is my prayer number 8:
put an end to hurt and hate.

This is my prayer number 9:
let the light of kindness shine.

This is my prayer number 10:
bring me safe to bed again.

THE STRAIGHT AND NARROW

6

I will choose the narrow path,
I will walk the straight,
Through the wide and winding world
Up to heaven's gate.

7

Quietly, in the morning,
I rise and look at the sky
To watch the darkness scatter
As sunlight opens the sky.
The day lies clear before me,
All fresh and shining and new,
And then I ask God to guide me
In all that I have to do.

8

I am a pilgrim
on a journey
to the place
where God is found;
every step
along that journey
is upon
God's holy ground.

9

Dear God,
I resolve this day to do what is right,
even if no one else will join me.

Lord, make us to walk in your way:
"Where there is love and wisdom,
there is neither fear nor ignorance;
where there is patience and humility,
there is neither anger nor annoyance;
where there is poverty and joy,
there is neither greed nor avarice;
where there is peace and contemplation,
there is neither care nor restlessness;
where there is the fear of God to guard
   the dwelling,
there no enemy can enter;
where there is mercy and prudence,
there is neither excess nor harshness";
this we know through your Son,
Jesus Christ our Lord.

St Francis of Assisi (1181–1226)

Growing good

II

I wash my hands
to make them clean
and ready to do good.

And God above
will teach me how
to do the things I should.

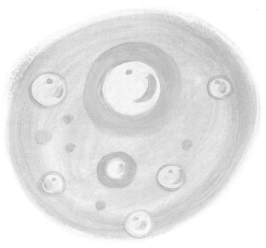

O God, make me good.
Make me wise.
Make me hardworking.
Make me honest.
Make me tactful.
Make me generous.
Make me truthful.
Make me loyal.
But most of all,
dear God,
make me your child.

BASED ON PROVERBS

13

I pray for the person I see in the mirror,
who's really a lot like me;
who needs to grow older and wiser and kinder
to be the best they can be.

14

Little deeds of kindness,
Little words of love,
Help to make earth happy,
Like the heaven above.

Julia Carney (1823–1908)

15

May my life shine
like a star in the night,
filling my world
with goodness and light.

16

We can do no great things,
Only small things with great love.

MOTHER TERESA OF CALCUTTA (1910–97)

17

May all my deeds
be wheat
not weeds.

TRULY SORRY

18

Mischief: it spreads like a bramble
Misdeeds: they wound like the thorn
And it takes so long
To put right each wrong
And that's why I'm feeling forlorn.

When I am in a temper
When I get really mad
I can be very dangerous
I can be very bad.

I'm wild as a tiger
I'm wild as a bear
I'm wilder than a wildebeest
And I don't even care.

Dear God who made the tiger
Dear God who made the bear
Please let me know you love me still
And that you'll always care.

MARK ROBINSON

20

Accidents will happen, Lord,
And things that spill will stain
So help me not to have
These silly accidents again.

21

I am sorry
and ashamed;
I will not
do THAT again.

22

Dear God,
For the silly things I have done wrong
I am sorry.

For the serious things I have done wrong
I am sorry.

For the things I didn't even know were wrong
I am sorry.

For all the things I need to put right
Make me strong.

MAKING AMENDS

23

I confess to you, O Lord,
all that I have done wrong.
Speak your forgiveness
into my heart
and help me to make
a new beginning.

24

O God, there is some mischief in me, deep as a dandelion root and bringing forth a thousand little seeds of naughtiness.

Turn that mischief into kindliness to produce a million good deeds and more.

25

Making amends
is an uphill road
and stony is the way.
At the top of the hill
you will find the gate
to a bright new shining day.

26

Dear God,
Help me to forget my
mistakes but to remember
what they taught me.

27

Dear God,
I would like something really
nasty to happen to my enemies…
unless you have a better idea.

28

Dear God,
I am not ready to forgive
but I am ready to be made ready.

29

Dear God,
Give us the courage to overcome
anger with love.

How to forgive:

Take one grudge
and drop it in the deep pond
  of forgetting.
Wait a while.

Within each ugly grudge
is the seed of forgiveness
and it will grow into the tree of peace.

THINKING OF OTHERS

31

We share the earth
we share the sky
we share the shining sea
with those we trust
with those we fear:
we are God's family.

32

Open my eyes
so I can see
the ways I could
more useful be.

Give me the strength
and heart and mind
to do the things
that are good and kind.

33

O God,
May I face every task
with courage and cheerfulness.

34

Love is giving, not taking,
mending, not breaking,
trusting, believing,
never deceiving,
patiently bearing
and faithfully sharing
each joy, every sorrow,
today and tomorrow.

ANONYMOUS

Dear God,
When I see someone in trouble, may I know when
to stop and help and when to hurry to fetch help;
but may I never pass by, pretending I did not see.

BASED ON JESUS' PARABLE OF THE GOOD SAMARITAN,
LUKE 10:25–37

O God,
We are all strangers in this world
and we are all travelling to your country.

So may we not treat anyone as a
    foreigner or an outsider,
but simply as a fellow human being
made in your image.

At home

37

Bless the window
Bless the door
Bless the ceiling
Bless the floor
Bless this place which is our home
Bless us as we go and come.

38

The circle of my family,
the circle of my friends
are safe within the circle
of the love that never ends.

Dear God, bless those who visit us: family, friends and strangers. May we make our home a place of love and kindness for all. May we share the things we have with generosity and cheerfulness.

VICTORIA TEBBS

40

Dear God,
I gratefully bow my head
To thank you for my daily bread,
And may there be a goodly share
On every table everywhere. Amen.

Mennonite children's prayer

41

For health and strength
and daily food,
we praise your name,
O Lord.

Traditional

42

Each time we eat,
may we remember God's love.

ANONYMOUS

43

We are hungry,
We have food,
We are family,
God is good.

SCHOOLDAYS

44

I am only me, but I'm still someone.
I cannot do everything, but I can do something.
Just because I cannot do everything does not give
   me the right to do nothing.

Motto from an Amish school

45

If our school were in heaven,
we would sweep the paths clean.

If our school were in heaven,
we would cultivate its garden.

If our school were in heaven,
we would keep our things neat.

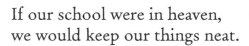

If our school were in heaven,
we would display our work for the angels to see.

If our school were in heaven,
we would treat everyone as a child of God.

So, here on earth, we will do these things
and so make our school more like heaven.

46

I've had a bad day at school, dear God,
An ever so very bad day;
You'd hardly believe how bad it was:
Just take those bad memories away.

And then let me start again, dear God,
And may my tomorrow be good;
You've got to believe how hard I'll try
To do all the things that I should.

47

Start each day with a fresh beginning,
as if this whole world was made anew.

MOTTO FROM AN AMISH SCHOOL

48

Bless to me, O God,
the work of my hands.
Bless to me, O God,
the work of my mind.
Bless to me, O God,
the work of my heart.

Anonymous

Holidays

49

Thank you, dear God,
for summer days
and summer adventures
and summer holidays so long
it seems that life will go on for ever.

O God, you have counted each grain of the sand
and the shells that lie washed on the shore.
Please keep us all safe, as if holding your hand
through this day, through this week, evermore.

The waves roll in from the glittering green
   of the sparkling summertime sea.
They curl and unfurl on the golden sand
   and run up the beach to me.

The waves roll out to the beautiful blue
   where the ocean touches the sky.
They swish and they slide with the silver tide
   and shyly they say goodbye.

Dear God, make me brave to explore
new paths.

53

My journey may be fast or
my journey may be slow;
may God be always with me
wherever I may go.

54

Father, lead us through this day
As we travel on our way.
Be our safety, be our friend,
Bring us to our journey's end.

PEOPLE OF THE WORLD

55

May all the peoples of the world have a place
where they can make their home.
May they live without quarrel.
May they live without enmity.
May they live in freedom and prosper.

FROM GENESIS 26

Where the bombs are falling
let there be only rain.

Where the bullets are whistling
let there be only wind.

Where war has left the land bleak and bare
let there be a springtime of peace.

Lord, watch over refugees:
tired feet aching.
Help them bear their heavy loads:
bent backs breaking.
May they find a place of rest:
no fears awake them.
May you always be their guide:
never forsake them.

58

Lord, help those who plant and sow,
weed and water, rake and hoe,
toiling in the summer heat
for the food they need to eat.

Bless the work of their tired hands:
turn their dry and dusty lands
to a garden, green and gold,
as their harvest crops unfold.

59

We see people in need
and do not know how to help.

The problem seems too big.
The problem seems too far.
The problem seems too dangerous.

Show us how to begin to help
in little ways.

ALL THINGS BRIGHT
AND BEAUTIFUL

60

If you have heard
the sound of birdsong
in the morning air,
then you will know
that heaven's music
reaches everywhere.

Thank you for the little things
we notice every day
that shine on earth
with heaven's gold
and cheer us on our way.

62

Grant me riches
here on earth –
things that are
of priceless worth:

The shining sun
the silver sea
the diamond rain
the emerald tree.

For better far
than any gold
these treasures are
that none can hold.

63

Who would make a tiny flower
so beautiful? It lasts an hour!
The bloom then quickly fades away
before the setting of the day.

Who would make a tiny leaf
so intricate? Its life is brief:
a season in the summer sun
before its fluttering life is done.

The One who made both great and small,
who loves and cares for one and all
on land and water, sky and sea:
the One who loves and cares for me.

64

Looking at the sky
while a tall tree sways
I hear God speaking
in a thousand different ways:
of melodies and miracles
that all are born on earth;
of dreams and possibilities
of everlasting worth.

ALL CREATURES GREAT AND SMALL

65

All things bright and beautiful,
All creatures great and small,
All things wise and wonderful,
The Lord God made them all.

CECIL FRANCES ALEXANDER (1818–95)

Multicoloured animals
With stripes and dots and patches:
God made each one different –
There isn't one that matches.

I think of the diverse majesty
of all of the creatures on earth:
some with the power to terrify
and others that only bring mirth.
I think of their shapes and their colours,
their secret and curious ways
and long for the words and the melody
to sing their Great Maker's praise.

68

Thank you, God, for birds that sing
from high up in the trees;
thank you for the butterflies
that dance upon the breeze.
Thank you for the wild beasts
of every stripe and hue.
Thank you for the whole round globe
of green and gold and blue.

Thank you, God, for lobsters
and the strange things of the sea.
Thank you for the insects –
the mosquito and the flea.
Thank you for the frogs and toads,
and bright-eyed things that lurk
among the ooze and mud and slime
and long-neglected murk.

Around the seasons

69

I will remember the buds of spring
When summertime leaves are green;

I will remember their rippling shade
When colours of autumn are seen;

I will remember the red and the gold
When wintertime branches are bare;

I will give thanks to the God of the trees
Whose love reaches everywhere.

70

The world has turned to greentime,
The trees are dressed in lace
And birds do sing
Of life and spring
And God's eternal grace.

71

The woods are God's own cathedral
with pillars that reach to the sky
and a faraway ceiling of fluttering leaves
where songbirds and angels fly.

72

All around the seasons
another year has flown.
Now it is my birthday
and look how I have grown.
All throughout the seasons
I celebrate each day
with everyone who loves me
and God to guide my way.

73

We plough the land,
God sends the rain
to bring the harvest
once again;
and when the fields
of wheat turn gold,
then God's great goodness
must be told.

BASED ON PSALM 65

74

Now the wind is coming,
Now the wind is strong,
Now the winter freezes
And the darkness will be long.
Now we see the starlight
In the midnight sky,
We know God is with us
And the angels are close by.

CHRISTMAS

75

Let us travel to Christmas
By the light of a star.
Let us go to the hillside
Right where the shepherds are.
Let us see shining angels
Singing from heaven above.
Let us see Mary cradling
God's holy child with love.

Away in a manger, no crib for a bed,
The little Lord Jesus laid down his sweet head.
The stars in the bright sky looked down where
   he lay,
The little Lord Jesus asleep on the hay.

The cattle are lowing, the baby awakes,
But little Lord Jesus no crying he makes.
I love thee, Lord Jesus! Look down from the sky,
And stay by my side until morning is nigh.

Be near me, Lord Jesus; I ask thee to stay
Close by me for ever, and love me, I pray.
Bless all the dear children in thy tender care,
And fit us for heaven, to live with thee there.

TRADITIONAL

Angels sang the Christmas news
To shepherds by their fold:
As we share
With love and care
The message still is told.

78

The wise men read the night-time sky
and now we read their story
of how they found the prince of peace,
newborn from heaven's glory.

We come, as if to Bethlehem,
to offer gifts of love
to make this world at Christmas time
a piece of heaven above.

79

The stars that shine at Christmas
Shine on throughout the year;
Jesus, born so long ago,
Still gathers with us here.
We listen to his stories,
We learn to say his prayer,
We follow in his footsteps
And learn to love and share.

Let there be little Christmases throughout
   the year,
when unexpected acts of kindness
bring heaven to earth.

JESUS, FRIEND OF LITTLE CHILDREN

81

Jesus, friend of little children,
  Be a friend to me;
Take my hand, and ever keep me
  Close to thee.

Never leave me, nor forsake me;
  Ever be my friend;
For I need thee, from life's dawning
  To its end.

WALTER J. MATHAMS (1851–1931)

Our Father in heaven,
hallowed be your name,
your kingdom come,
your will be done,
on earth as in heaven.
Give us today our daily bread.
Forgive us our sins
as we forgive those who sin against us.
Lead us not into temptation
but deliver us from evil.

For the kingdom, the power,
and the glory are yours
now and for ever.
Amen

THE PRAYER JESUS TAUGHT

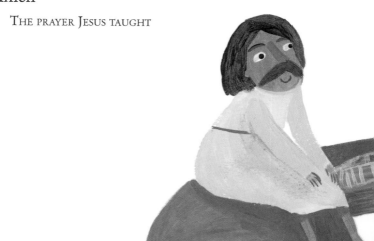

Jesus loves me! This I know,
For the Bible tells me so.
Little ones to Him belong;
They are weak, but He is strong.

CHORUS:
Yes, Jesus loves me!
Yes, Jesus loves me!
Yes, Jesus loves me!
The Bible tells me so.

Jesus loves me! This I know,
As He loved so long ago,
Taking children on His knee,
Saying, "Let them come to Me."

CHORUS

Jesus loves me still today,
Walking with me on my way,
Wanting as a friend to give
Light and love to all who live.

ANNA B. WARNER (1827–1915)

84

Jesus bids us shine
With a pure, clear light,
Like a little candle
Burning in the night;
In this world of darkness,
So we must shine,
You in your small corner,
And I in mine.

ANONYMOUS

Easter and Pentecost

85

In the Easter garden
the leaves are turning green;
in the Easter garden
the risen Lord is seen.

In the Easter garden
we know that God above
brings us all to heaven
through Jesus and his love.

86

There is a green hill far away,
  Without a city wall,
Where the dear Lord was crucified
  Who died to save us all.

We may not know, we cannot tell,
  What pains he had to bear,
But we believe it was for us
  He hung and suffered there.

He died that we might be forgiven,
  He died to make us good;
That we might go at last to heaven,
  Saved by his Precious Blood.

There was no other good enough
  To pay the price of sin;
He only could unlock the gate
  Of heaven, and let us in.

O, dearly, dearly has he loved,
  And we must love him too,
And trust in his redeeming Blood,
  And try his works to do.

CECIL FRANCES ALEXANDER (1818–95)

87

Friday sunset, black and red.
Weep, for Jesus Christ is dead.

Sunday sunrise, white and gold.
Christ is risen, as foretold.

88

The tree of thorns
is dressed in white
for resurrection day;
and joy springs from
the underworld
now death is put away.

89

Let the Spirit come
like the winds that blow:
take away my doubts;
help my faith to grow.

Let the Spirit come
like a flame of gold:
warm my soul within;
make me strong and bold.

Harvest thanksgiving

90

Harvest of leaf,
Harvest of fruit,
Harvest of stem,
Harvest of root;
Harvest of lowland,
Harvest of hill,
Harvest that all
May eat their fill.

We plough the fields, and scatter
The good seed on the land.
But it is fed and watered
By God's almighty hand.
He sends the snow in winter,
The warmth to swell the grain,
The breezes and the sunshine,
And soft refreshing rain:
All good gifts around us
Are sent from heaven above;
Then thank the Lord, O thank the Lord,
For all his love.

MATTHIAS CLAUDIUS (1740–1815)

92

The Lord is good to me,
And so I thank the Lord
For giving me the things I need,
The sun, the rain, the appleseed.
The Lord is good to me.

ATTRIBUTED TO JOHN CHAPMAN (1774–1845)

93

The harvest of our garden
is astonishingly small;
but oh, dear God, we thank you
that there's anything at all.

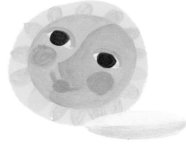

94

The harvests have ripened in the sun;
There's plenty of food for everyone:
There's some for ourselves and more to share
With all of God's people everywhere.

PSALMS

95

I praise the Lord with all my soul,
my strength, my heart, my mind:
he blesses me with love and grace
and is for ever kind.

<small>BASED ON PSALM 103:1–4</small>

Praise the Lord from heaven,
all beings of the height!
Praise him, holy angels
and golden sun so bright.

Praise him, silver moonlight,
praise him, every star!
Let your praises shine
throughout the universe so far.

Praise the Lord from earth below,
all beings of the deep!
Lightning, flash! You thunder, roar!
You ocean creatures, leap.

Praise him, hill and mountain!
Praise him, seed and tree.
Praise him, all you creatures
that run the wide world free.

Let the mighty praise him.
Let the children sing.
Men and women, young and old:
praise your God and king.

FROM PSALM 148

97

Praise the Lord with trumpets –
all praise to him belongs;
praise him with your music,
your dancing and your songs!

BASED ON PSALM 150

98

Dear God, you are my shepherd,
You give me all I need,
You take me where the grass grows green
And I can safely feed.

You take me where the water
Is quiet and cool and clear;
And there I rest and know I'm safe
For you are always near.

Based on Psalm 23

99

The earth may shake, the mountains fall,
the seas may rage and roar:
God is my shelter and my strength
for now and evermore.

Based on Psalm 46

Bible verses to know by heart

100

Jesus said:

"Love the Lord your God with all your heart, with all your soul, and with all your mind." This is the greatest and the most important commandment.

The second most important commandment is like it:
"Love your neighbour as you love yourself."

The whole Law of Moses and the teachings of the prophets depend on these two commandments.

Matthew 22:37–40

Jesus said:

You have heard that it was said, "Love your friends, hate your enemies." But now I tell you: love your enemies and pray for those who persecute you, so that you may become the children of your Father in heaven.

MATTHEW 5:43–45

Jesus said:

And now I give you a new commandment: love one another. As I have loved you, so you must love one another. If you have love for one another, then everyone will know that you are my disciples.

JOHN 13:34–35

Love is patient and kind; it is not jealous or conceited or proud; love is not ill-mannered or selfish or irritable; love does not keep a record of wrongs; love is not happy with evil, but is happy with the truth. Love never gives up; and its faith, hope, and patience never fail. Love is eternal.

Meanwhile these three remain: faith, hope, and love; and the greatest of these is love.

PAUL'S FIRST LETTER TO THE CORINTHIANS, 13:4–8, 13

104

Dear friends, let us love one another, because love comes from God. Whoever loves is a child of God and knows God. Whoever does not love does not know God, for God is love. And God showed his love for us by sending his only Son into the world, so that we might have life through him.

<small>THE FIRST LETTER OF JOHN, 4:7–9</small>

105

Let the Spirit direct your lives...
The Spirit produces love, joy, peace, patience, kindness, goodness, faithfulness, humility, and self-control.

<small>PAUL'S LETTER TO THE GALATIANS, 5:16, 22–23</small>

106

In days to come…
God will settle disputes among great nations.
They will hammer their swords into ploughs
and their spears into pruning knives.
Nations will never again go to war,
never prepare for battle again.

ISAIAH 2:2, 4

107

Hope returns when I remember this one thing:
The Lord's unfailing love and mercy still continue,
Fresh as the morning, as sure as the sunrise.

LAMENTATIONS 3:21–23

DIFFICULT DAYS

108

O God,
be to me
like the evergreen tree
and shelter me in your shade,
and bless me again
like the warm gentle rain
that gives life to all you have made.

BASED ON HOSEA 14:4–8

109

Deeply gloomy
Deeply sad
When the day
Goes deeply bad.

Deeply hoping
God above
Will enfold me
In his love.

In my distress, O Lord, I called to you.

Deep in the troubled waters, I called to you.

Wrapped in the slime of the sea, I called to you.

Down by the gates of the dead, I called to you.

In my distress, O Lord, I called to you,
and you answered me.

BASED ON JONAH'S PRAYER, JONAH 2

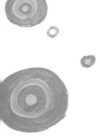

III

In my bed
and feeling rotten,
bored and gloomy
and forgotten.

May the angels
in the sky
watch to check
I do not die.

May the angels
here on land
come and hold me
by the hand.

112

Feeling poorly in my bed,
Feeling poorly in my head,
Feeling poorly, feeling pain:
God, please make me well again.

113

A prayer for winter sniffles
A prayer for winter sneezes
A prayer said in a croaky voice
With little grunts and wheezes.

WHEN GOODBYE IS FOR EVER

114

Every day
in silence we remember

those whom we loved
to whom we have said a last goodbye.

Every day
in silence we remember.

115

May kind earth take the body,
May heaven take the soul;
And though our hearts are broken,
May God soon make them whole.

116

Lead me through the darkness
where I cannot see my way;
make a path for me to walk
into the light of day.

117

Bless the autumn leaves that fall
and crumble in decay;
may the trees of heaven bloom
in everlasting day.

118

In heaven's streets
the cherry trees
are hung with blossoms white;
And you'll be there
for cherry-time
if you would live aright.

119

A prayer for little tiny things
whose little life has flown:
may they be safe in God's great love –
they are God's very own.

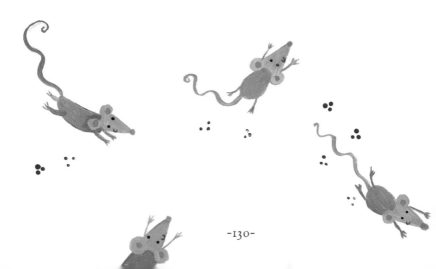

120

When little creatures die
And it's time to say goodbye
To a bright-eyed furry friend,
We know that God above
Will remember them with love:
A love that will never end.

AND SO TO BED

121

Day is done,
Gone the sun
From the lake,
From the hills,
From the sky.
Safely rest,
All is well!
God is nigh.

ANONYMOUS

122

Now the day is over,
  Night is drawing nigh.
Shadows of the evening
  Steal across the sky.

Now the darkness gathers,
  Stars begin to peep,
Birds and beasts and flowers
  Soon will be asleep.

Jesu, give the weary
  Calm and sweet repose;
With thy tenderest blessing
  May our eyelids close.

Through the long night-watches
  May thine Angels spread
Their white wings above me,
  Watching round my bed.

When the morning wakens,
  Then may I arise,
Pure, and fresh, and sinless
  In thy holy eyes.

Glory to the Father,
  Glory to the Son,
And to thee, blest Spirit
  Whilst all ages run.

SABINE BARING-GOULD (1834–1924)

123

The sun descending in the west,
The evening star does shine,
The birds are silent in their nest,
And I must seek for mine.

The moon, like a flower,
In heaven's high bower,
With silent delight
Sits and smiles on the night.

WILLIAM BLAKE (1757–1827)

124

The moon shines clear as silver,
The sun shines bright like gold,
And both are very lovely,
And very, very old.

God hung them up as lanterns,
For all beneath the sky;
And nobody can blow them out,
For they are up too high.

Charlotte Druitt Cole

GOD BLESS US ALL

125

God bless all those that I love;
God bless all those that love me;
God bless all those that love those
  that I love,
And all those that love those that
  love me.

FROM A SAMPLER

126

Dear God, bless all my family,
as I tell you each name;
and please bless each one differently
for no one's quite the same.

127

Tucked up in my little bed,
I say a little prayer
For all the people in this house
And people everywhere.

God bless Gran
through the sunlit day.
God bless Gran
through the starlit night.
God bless Gran
when we are together.
God bless Gran
when we're out of sight.

129

May the Lord bless you,
may the Lord take care of you;
May the Lord be kind to you,
may the Lord be gracious to you;
May the Lord look on you with favour,
may the Lord give you peace.

FROM NUMBERS 6:24–26

130

I see the moon,
And the moon sees me;
God bless the moon
And God bless me.

TRADITIONAL

131

The moon shines bright,
The stars give light
Before the break of day;
God bless you all
Both great and small
And send a joyful day.

TRADITIONAL

IN THE CHARGE OF AN ANGEL

132

Angel of God,
my guardian dear
to whom God's love
commits me here,
ever this day
be at my side
to light and guard,
to rule and guide.

TRADITIONAL

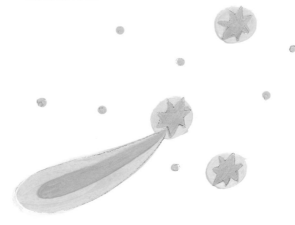

Matthew, Mark, Luke and John,
Bless the bed that I lie on.
Before I lay me down to sleep,
I pray the Lord my soul to keep.

Four corners to my bed,
Four angels there are spread,
Two at the foot, two at the head:
Four to carry me when I'm dead.

I go by sea, I go by land,
The Lord made me with his right hand.
Should any danger come to me,
Sweet Jesus Christ deliver me.

He's the branch and I'm the flower,
Pray God send me a happy hour,
And should I die before I wake,
I pray the Lord my soul to take.

TRADITIONAL

134

From ghoulies and ghosties
Long-leggety beasties
And things that go bump in the night,
Good Lord deliver us.

Traditional Cornish prayer

135

Lord, keep us safe this night,
Secure from all our fears;
May angels guard us while we sleep,
Till morning light appears.

JOHN LELAND (1754–1841)

136

Cradle me, kind angels, in a coracle
   of darkness
Float me on the starry silver sea
Let me drift away through the waves
   of cloud and grey
To the land where bright morning
   waits for me.

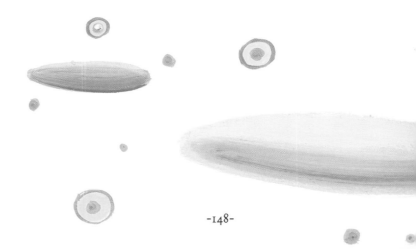

137

A silver moon
A velvet sky:
May the angels
Watch close by.

A velvet sky
A silver moon:
May I fall asleep
Quite soon.

GOODNIGHT

138

Good night! Good night!
Far flies the light;
But still God's love
Shall flame above,
Making all bright.
Good night! Good night!

VICTOR HUGO (1802–85)

The lightning and thunder
They go and they come;
But the stars and the stillness
Are always at home.

GEORGE MACDONALD (1824–1905)

140

I give you the end of a golden string,
  Only wind it into a ball,
It will lead you in at Heaven's gate
  Built in Jerusalem's wall.

WILLIAM BLAKE (1757–1827)

141

I call to God for help
and God answers me.

I lie down to sleep
and God protects me.

FROM PSALM 3

142

Be thou a bright flame before me,
Be thou a guiding star above me,
Be thou a smooth path below me,
And a kindly shepherd behind me,
Today, tonight, and for ever.

FROM CARMINA GADELICA

143

Deep peace of the running waves to you,
Deep peace of the flowing air to you,
Deep peace of the quiet earth to you,
Deep peace of the shining stars to you,
Deep peace of the shades of night to you,
Moon and stars always giving light to you,
Deep peace of Christ, the Son of Peace, to you.

TRADITIONAL GAELIC BLESSING

144

The peace of joy,
The peace of light,
The peace of day,
The peace of night.

145

Glory to thee, my God, this night,
For all the blessings of the light;
Keep me, O keep me, King of kings,
Beneath thine everlasting wings.

Praise God from whom all blessings flow;
Praise him, all creatures here below;
Praise him above, ye heavenly host;
Praise Father, Son, and Holy Ghost.

BISHOP THOMAS KEN (1637–1711)

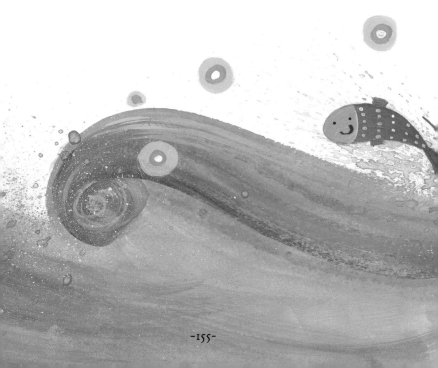

INDEX OF FIRST LINES

Numbers refer to prayer numbers.